SOUL REFRACTION

PAUL R KOHN

Copyright

 Published by Dragonfly Publishing, February 2023
© All rights reserved by the author

This book is copyright. Apart from any fair dealing for the purpose of private study, research, criticism or review, as permitted under the Copyright Act, no part may be reproduced by any process without written permission from the publisher.

Because of the dynamic nature of the Internet, any web addresses or links contained in this book may have changed since publication and may no longer be valid.

 A catalogue record for this work is available from the National Library of Australia

ISBN (sc): 978-0-6455953-0-7
ISBN (e): 978-0-6455953-1-4

Cover artwork: ©Neshka Turner. *Soul Refraction*. 2022
Forest artwork: ©Neshka Turner. *Tree*. 2022
Memory artwork: ©Neshka Turner. *Face1*. 2022
Innocence Scorned artwork: ©Neshka Turner. *Petals*. 2022
Ignition Potential artwork: ©Neshka Turner. *Face2*. 2022
Jolt artwork: ©Neshka Turner. *Clock*. 2022
Favourite Song artwork: ©Neshka Turner. *Viola*. 2022
From Dad, With Love artwork: ©Neshka Turner. *Father*. 2022

DEDICATION

This is for everyone who has ever felt unseen, unheard, lost or broken, either now or at any point in their life.

This is for the people who believe in me and support me each and every day.

This is for the people who support the words I share, both written and spoken, online, live, and now here in these pages.

This is for the people who believed in me who are no longer here, either by choice or not...

I truly value, appreciate, love you all, and will hold space for you forever.

I am always, always here, and I hope that my words touch you, support you, help your soul to find understanding, to heal, to grow, to soar.

PROLOGUE

Life is a journey... A trajectory of ups and downs, lefts and rights, light and dark. A soul refraction...

Soul Refraction is those moments we are consumed with dark feelings... Hurt, shame, guilt... It's the moments that we are broken, vulnerable, exposed, alone, invisible. And it's the things we do both in and out of those moments to survive, the way we reflect, repair, rebuild, regrow to turn it around, shine a light in the darkness to help ourselves and others. Light ourselves up and, in doing so, light up the world to show that these things can be overcome. That we can survive, heal, grow, and positively impact the body, mind, heart, soul and spirit of ourselves, and in doing so, positively impact others too.

To help every soul to shine, to soar.

There have been so many experiences I have gone through, endured, most of which I ignored for a long time... Until I went through something that dragged everything up from the trenches. Something that broke me in ways I never imagined I could break. It showed me the best and worst of myself and others. It showed me my own shortcomings, the stigma and isolation of mental illness as I navigated PTSD (Post-Traumatic Stress Disorder) and MDD (Major Depressive Disorder), and the shortcomings of the mental health care system.

It has been the hardest and loneliest journey I have ever embarked on. It nearly broke me beyond repair. Nearly...

But it didn't.

I faced my demons head on and survived. Something I never take for granted.

I am torn apart by wounds and bruises, held together by scars and stitches, but despite everything, I am uniquely me. And I share my journey in the hope that it helps someone, saves someone, gives someone a new perspective. I shine my light in the darkness so others feel seen, heard, understood, and know that they are not alone, know that they too have power even when they feel powerless.

And that's why I write and share poetry.

Because even in commonality, we each have our own unique story.

Because each of us are a unique work of art!

CONTENTS
1 - SOUL BREAK

Poet or Poetry	1
Trauma	3
Cascading Sleeplessness	6
Forest	7
Sleep-waking	8
Death	9
Silence	12
Connection Protection	13
Trapped	15
Broken	16
Struggle	17
Dog (Dead on Ground)	19
Lungs	20
Hanging on Hope	21
Poison	22
Cost Reward	23
Waves	25
Consistently Inconsistent	28
Worthless	29
Reality is Shifting	32
Anxiety Pandemic	33
White wash	35
Bang!	36
Unworthy	37
Chaos	39
Memory	40
Push On	41
Sorry	42
Visibly Invisible	43
In the End	44
Heal to Hear	45

2 - SOUL HEAL

Ghosts	49
Burden	50
PTSD and MDD	51
Stone	56
Circling - A Day in the Life...	57
Not Alone	59
When	62
Bleeding Heart	63
Go	65
What is this?	67
Good Bad	68
Lost and Found	69
Public Silence	70
Where Did You Go?	71
Silent Screams	73
Missing	74
Innocence Scorned	75
Fearless	77
Wake Up	79
Quarter Turn	80
Strong	81
Adapt	83
Fall Away	85
Caught By A Dream	87
Ignition Potential	88
I Am Art	89

3 - SOUL GROW

Mind vs Heart	93
Pick Me Up	95
Clock	96
Jolt	97
Storm	98
Looking Forward Back	99
Noose	101
Want	102
Walk The Talk	103
Hands Down	106
Favourite Song	107
Beached	110
Cleanse	111
Change	112
Reflection	113
Future	114

4 - SOUL SOAR

In the Room Where I Belong	117
New Beginnings	118
Speck	119
Re-Create	120
Why Words?	121
Journey	122
Souled	123
Promise	124
Journey of the Souled	125
Twin Flame	127
Breathe You In	128
You. Beautiful you	129
Precious Pieces	132
Hidden	133
Cusp	134
Home	135
Courage	136
Rise	137
Songtensity	138
From Dad, With Love	139
Grounding	141
You Are Seen	143
Survival	145
May Your Future	146

Notes
Acknowledgements
About The Author

1 - SOUL BREAK

"Trauma is a relentless beast with sharp claws that tears at your heart and soul, with fangs that constantly gnaw on your mind."

POET OR POETRY

Hello. My name's Paul, and this is my artist statement…

Kind of…
Not really…
It'll have to do.

I am a poet. At least, I call myself one.
It's like an alcoholic, except I consume an excess of words, of ideas, of thoughts, of emotions, only to reach my tipping point and regurgitate them out onto the page through my hand with a pen.
Hopefully in a way that makes sense to me, hopefully in a way that makes sense to you, hopefully in a way that helps someone, saves someone!

I seek to learn from every encounter and experience in my life, good or bad.
From the time I was born, to the moment I find myself in now.
Like the time I played a piano and was good at it, to the time I played a guitar and was okay at that too. If an instrument has strings, I'll try and play it, and I'll probably sing along too.
Like the time I wrote poems and called them lyrics, to the time I wrote lyrics and called it poetry.

Like the time I was glassed and bled shards from my back, stitched myself with sticky tape and bandaged myself, burying the superficial wounds and the emotional wounds all at once.

To the time I was mugged and left in the gutter unconscious, battered and bruised. Crying out in pain, in shame, in the relentlessness of all that surfaced. Only to be made mute, left broken, discarded, alone, empty.

Learning that each and every scar, whether seen or not, has a story to tell.
Often more than one story.
And each and every story I have to tell, I turn into art to help others feel seen and heard.
Because I know firsthand what it's like to not be.
Because in my darkest moments, I know firsthand what it's like to feel abandoned, worthless, invisible.
And that's why I write poetry...

So, on reflection...

Hello. My name is Paul, and I thought I was a poet, but now I realise I am the poem itself.

TRAUMA

My feet drag as I walk the many, many miles alone. My tongue trails along behind, like a dead weight. Its ability to speak and be truly heard taken away through silence and exhaustion, judgement and shame.

Any sense of worth I had at this time of worthlessness disappears in a heartbeat, taken away right when I needed to grasp it with all that I am.

Brutal experiences, both new and old, have caused a trauma and depression in me like I have never felt or spiralled down before, bringing me closer to the edge than I have ever, ever been. And in that, I have held on too tightly to the only people in my life who are right and true and real; my reactions to my own triggers ultimately hurting them, triggering them... I will never forgive myself for this, for I never wanted to hurt them… And this knowing that I have further affects my reactions, adds to my triggers, feeds my trauma…

But that's the thing with trauma; it's so misunderstood... Parts of your brain that just never should switch off shut down completely, and the parts that should be mostly silent become loudly hyperactive and kick everything up a notch, taking away your control, your rationale.

My psych draws a picture of an oversized baked bean on an orange piece of paper and says it's my brain. She draws three more circles inside, crosses two out, and explains what is working and what isn't; why I am reacting to triggers like I am and why I am powerless to stop it.

She says none of this is my fault.

I say, "Thanks…"
But it all feels like my fault, just the same.

I cry; harder than I have ever cried in my life. The brutality of recent experiences and the surfacing of old ones has been hard enough to handle. I have lost so much as I've spiralled. But, in this moment, to come to the realisation I have hurt the most important people in my life is more confronting and painful than any of it!

I tell my psych this, and she gives me a couple of strategies to try and keep my reactions in control when I feel triggered; I try them, and they work, but at the same time, they internalise everything even more, and so while I don't react outwardly when triggered, internally I am more broken than ever; a babbling tearful mess when alone. Carrying a mind that is never quiet, a heart that is broken, a soul that is crushed.

And I am alone a lot, for it is not only the most important people in my life I have inadvertently hurt and unintentionally pushed away but other friends and family too…
Because I have held on too tightly or shut down too hard…

Because I've been too much or not enough…

[cont…]

Trauma is not something to be taken lightly. Trauma is misunderstood in so many ways, even by those who have experienced it before. Trauma hits and affects everyone differently. Trauma does not always instantly reveal how it is going to impact you. Trauma is a relentless beast with sharp claws that tears at your heart and soul, with fangs that constantly gnaw on your mind. Trauma, indeed, any mental health condition, can't be seen like a physical injury. It's not something that is easily recognised, and because of this, people blame you or turn away and abandon you instead of showing compassion and understanding, the cost of which is far greater than anyone can imagine to the person experiencing trauma.

And right when you need someone, through your own actions and reactions, you push them away harder in order to protect them. Or so you think.

It is a lonely, lonely place to be and one that can potentially cost you your life…

Not going to lie; it nearly cost me mine, but I was lucky. I can't explain how or why, but despite having pushed people away, they were holding me and protecting me that fateful night… Their souled presence physically saved me in a way I can't explain and filled me with the determination I needed to push on, to heal, to grow. Their souled presence, their voice, showed me that I am worth it.

I AM WORTH IT!

Cascading Sleeplessness

I lay awake staring at the ceiling,
watching my thoughts play out before my eyes.
The scene so vivid I could reach out and touch it.
Is it real or is it just a dream?

The silent movie I see above me,
keeps me on edge; what will happen next?
As sleep evades me once again,
I lay awake staring at the ceiling.

So vivid, it's like I'm actually moving,
walking, running from those things chasing me.
But it's pitch black around me, silent as I stare above,
watching my thoughts play out before my eyes.

I stumble, I fall; startled, my body shakes,
feels like the ground is actually scratching me.
I see a tree, crawl towards it to help me rise up,
the scene so vivid I could reach out and touch it.

Awake or asleep, I can no longer tell,
the cold sweat, the darkness, the silence feels like hell.
The exhaustion I feel, so heavy I can't move.
Is it real or is it just a dream?

FOREST

When a tree falls in the forest, does anyone hear it scream?
Or is it silenced just like me in my time of need?
Pointing to the sky until it can reach the sun no more,
crying out, cracking, as it falls to the forest floor.

See, in trauma I'm no different to that falling tree,
cos in this people forest, I am only heard by me.

SLEEP-WAKING

I cannot sleep, I cannot wake.

So I lay here wide asleep

dreaming only in black.

DEATH

Death; not dead... But a feeling like death. Did you choose this road, or did it choose you? Is paranoia hunting you? Is this your curse? Or is this your opportunity?

Opportunity...
Seen so much life, yet never really lived.
Seen so much death, yet never really died.
Loneliness. Heartache. Suffering. Pain. Every day is a total drain on your senses.
Does that make you desensitized? No!
Used. Abused. Beaten. Broken... Yet determined.

Determined...
The challenge... That is what this is...
To be the best you can be for everyone, despite how you yourself feel.
Light up other peoples' world at the expense of your own.
Bring a little light to their darkness. Bring a little healing to their pain. Bring a little direction to their confusion.
That is what you want to do. That is what makes you feel whole; feel purposeful.
That is what gives you the strength to keep going yourself...
That is what you hold on to, even when others around you let go. When they are there no more. When they give up caring.

Care...
You don't care what people think or say about you. You've heard it all before, dealt with it all before.
Life is too important for that. Relationships are too important for that.
They try to break you, but you are strong enough in yourself to not let them hurt you, but worried that they will hurt others. Others that you care too much about to see broken, distraught, destroyed.

Others...
Why are they so close in their time of need yet so far away in yours?
Why do they always take but rarely give?
Why do they do that to you when you want advice? When you need them most? When you are at your lowest?

Need...
And what is it that you need anyway? You've been doing this on your own for so long now that you're used to it, yet you still struggle.
Take some of your own advice, your own medicine, your own heart.
You can do it; you can take this on your own.
Even if it kills you, at least you'll die whole. Even if it hurts you, at least you made someone else feel different, feel brighter, feel better.

[cont...]

Better...

Where is your head really at? How do you get out of the rut you are in? How do you find the sense of freedom that you help others achieve?

Listen to yourself. Take your own advice. Don't overthink it... Understand it. Don't worry, just care.

Care about those around you, friend or foe. But always keep an extra close eye on the people you know.

Protect them with everything you have in every way you can every single day.

Make that your legacy...

SILENCE

The silence is deafening, slowly killing me…
And when the silence does break, it's my voice that is mute,
ignored.
Like I'm placed in a jar, lid tightly closed,
sealed in with no air.
Only when the jar is opened am I allowed to breathe,
catch my breath,
but the lid is replaced, sealed shut once again before any
words can escape my mouth,

My scream is silenced…

Left voiceless, I bury my thoughts, my emotions,
become numb in my futile existence.
I hurt myself to feel less pain, just to feel anything at all,
be less of a drain on my life and those around me,
who are few and far between…

Pushed away relentlessly, no second thought given, it's my
fault I'm left a shadow,
an empty shell of a boy, too broken to rise.
Clinging to a slither of hope with all that I am,
that someday soon,
one day, everything will be fine, everything will be alright,
everything will be as it should be, as it needs to be…

And just hoping like hell I survive long enough to see it.

CONNECTION PROTECTION

> "The human brain is wired for connection,
> but trauma rewires the brain for protection."

I read these words…
I tear up…
I feel the words bounce in my head over and over; a resounding echo I never wanted to hear.
I feel the punches, the scratches, the scars from the night I can't remember, the mugging I can't recall.
The waking that left me shaking and scared.
Oh SO scared…
I have never felt more terrified in my life than I did when I came to that night…
I have never felt guilt, felt shame, like I felt the next day, blaming only myself for a situation I had less than no control over.
But blaming myself nonetheless…
See, PTSD isn't always caused by something you remember; sometimes, it's caused by something you can't recall at all.
My dearest friend warned me that this moment in time, this night that I could not recall, could result in PTSD if I did not get help fast…
I heeded that warning, and I did so as fast as I could.
Just not fast enough…

I sit with my psych, talking of all it has done to me, all I have hurt, all I have lost.

I cry. Harder than I have ever cried before.

I am told none of this is my fault…

But that doesn't make it any easier…

It doesn't stop the things long suppressed being dragged up.

It doesn't stop the hurt I cause myself, that I inadvertently cause others.

Trauma is not something you bounce back from overnight. And even when it does feel like you're making headway, a simple sight, a sound, a smell, can take you a hundred thousand steps back.

TRAPPED

I cry out in my time of need,

But everyone is   out   of   reach.

Left silenced like a mime,

trapped in a box, a world I can't escape.

Just me and my mind,

taunting me.

BROKEN

The world I'm in seems far from here, a place as black as night,
and the candle I bring does nothing for my sight.
The air is thick in this place, so very hard to breathe,
the pound in my chest, my muscles spasm, causing me to seethe.

I'm broken, starting to decay.
Broken mind, broken soul; it's all slipping away.
I'm broken; the end's so far, I cannot reach.
Eyes are weeping, bodies shaking, the flood is unleashed.

Silence screaming, darkness blinding, the cold is starting to burn.
Full of emptiness is my soul-less soul, where the hell do I turn?
Embracing my head in my hands, there's no one here to see.
As I look into the mirror, I barely recognise it's me.

There's no one to turn to, no one to trust.
Trying to scratch my way out through a cage of rust.
Lashing out, hurting those closest to me.
Why can't my mind let me be, set me free.

STRUGGLE

The sense of helplessness overwhelms me as everything that could go wrong is doing just that, all at once.
My struggle in my time of need is invisible, ignored by everyone but me.
As I wonder where to go, what to do from here, I ponder how to make it through the day I find myself in,
When every single day is a struggle for survival...
Every morning has me hugging a lamp post at a dimly lit station
as the train approaches. But am I holding it? Or is it holding me?
Using its gravity to pull me near its solid, strong and firm footing on the platform,
grounding me more than I know, keeping me alive.

Abandoned by those who love me the most, left helpless, hopeless, useless, broken, empty.
Nothing but a burden to everyone I know; always too much, yet never enough.
Holding on strong but not knowing why; if not for my children, I would surely die.
Lost in everything I try to grasp, hold on to.
Told it would be better if I wasn't here, told that things are better now I am ignored, pushed away.
A shell of what I used to be to everyone in my life, if they even remember me.
Left helpless, hopeless and unattractive in every single sense of my being,
the struggle of this worthless man is real.

So where to from here? I don't have a clue; everything that was once stable is now not,
and everything that was already unstable is destroyed, seemingly beyond repair.
The sense of loss in every facet of my being breaks me as I bury everything as deeply as I can;
denied the right to respond, denied the right to feel.
The confusion and emotions are ripping me to shreds from the inside out,
the path to self-destruction is lit up like an airport runway.
And yet I push on as best I can, put on a brave face, try to push through each day and bring normality,
to what feels like a wasted, futile and numb existence.

But that is still better than the alternative, right?
And so I continue holding onto the hope that there is always hope. That things will be better tomorrow.

DOG (DEAD ON GROUND)

I feel your heart, feel your breath.
You dragged yourself here, minutes from death.
Others stopped, they're simply standing near
in shock; not talking, they seem scared in your fear.

One person who's helping is moved to tears
phoning everyone they can, to quell their fears.
Warning us all, "Don't go too near!"
Ignoring them, I touch you, let you know I'm here.

I talk to you, not stopping, trying to calm you down.
The rise and fall of your chest ceases, and I frown.
My tears break through, trying to find your beating heart.
You're gone now; I close your eyes, wonder how every end has a start.

Run home and grab a blanket to cover your empty shell.
Every step, every breath in this moment feels like hell.
I'm shaking, my eyes weep as your blood fills the gutter.
"Cover it up, help me move it!" I hear the policeman mutter.

Take you to the hospital to see what they can do.
Our fears confirmed; it's too late, too late for you.
I help lift your empty shell from the car.
Where are those who love you? Are they near or far?

The situation endures, it's taunting me
as I lie here now; attempting to dream.
The tears, the flashbacks come as I try to sleep.
The sights, the sounds, the sadness, I will always keep.

LUNGS

As I sink slowly, I hold my breath, brace myself for the pain

when I hit the bottom, aware that the fall will knock the air from my lungs,

from my body.

My heartbeat slows, as the last of the air is carried by my blood,

consumed by every extremity of my body in the hope of

keeping me alive.

Hitting the bottom with a thud, I push up, hope to break the surface

before the darkness consumes me, eats me alive. I rise against the pull,

reach for the light.

Gagging, gasping,
right before another wave smashes me to the bottom once again.

HANGING ON HOPE

Never give someone the power to destroy you.

I did once…

And I'm still suffering in silence.

Still mourning in distance.

Still paying for it every single day.

Cos love is a noose, and hope is a hangman!

And this hangman is here to stay…

POISON

Why do they see poison in me when it's only love I seek to be?

Why do I bother to hold on, to push on, to be strong,

when all I want to do is dig a hole and pull the soil blanket

over me?

LOST REWARD

Chewed up, spat out, kicked to the side of the road.
No one to see if I'm okay; I'm as I've always been, alone.
As I stand here, lost in the emotionless of my emotions, ribs ripped wide open,
my heart beats outside my chest; I can see it, a red mess.
Feel its irregular beat closing in around me, crushing my temples, causing my body to tense, making it oh so very hard to breathe.

I am nothing more than a passenger on this planet, a speck of dust in the universe in which we all exist.
Being sucked into a vacuum, spinning, my control is out of my control, held by everyone but me. Pulled left and right, through thick and thin, sold to the highest bidder who never ever pays.
The only one paying is me…

So, what of it? "You do alright," they say. "You'll be alright," they say.
But how the hell would they know when all they do is take, but never seek to know or understand what's crawling beneath my skin.
When scars are admired as battles won, but never recognised for the hurt and pain they represent.
When they always talk and tell, yet never ask, never seek to try to understand; to know me.

Yet there I always am at their beck-and-call, dropping everything to help them, to make sure they are okay, even if I'm not. To make sure they have what they need, even if it means I don't.

It's all I have ever known, whether I like it or not.
It's all I've ever been, whether it's convenient or not.

Sanity is my cost.

Self-sacrifice is my reward.

WAVES

As the wave of unworthiness hits me, all I believe in, all I hope for, is taken away in a heartbeat.
The shadow of self-doubt casts itself over my mind, my heart, my soul, ripping me apart.
I've been weak. I need to be stronger, more determined, more resilient, more silent.
Cos, while it's not about proving myself, it's all about proving myself; to myself, to those I value, to those I love.
Showing them that they're seen, they're heard, they're respected, and they deserve nothing less than that from me, even if it means they want less of me.
Showing them I have what it takes to be the best I can be for me and for them, always.

See, that's the thing about trauma, about the relentless depression that comes with it.
About all the darkness it drags up from the depths of your being.
About the shame.
About the guilt.
About the vulnerable invulnerability.
About the sleepless nights spent woken and the days spent walking around sleeping.
About the self-medication and the self-violation.
About the smile you wear to avoid the questions of despair.
About the "you'll be fines" and the "everything will be alrights."
About the...

How do you know what I'm thinking, what I'm feeling, what I'm going through when you're too busy telling me it's fine when it's not…

…

It's just not!

…

But that's assumptions, isn't it?
They make an ass of you and of me?

…

But I digress…
Because I'm not here to complain, I'm here to explain.
Because I've worked so damn hard to come back from the brink.
Because the journey isn't easy, and sometimes nor are the decisions.
Because sometimes, despite what you're told or what you think or what you feel, you have to step back.
You just have to step back. Take a deep breath. Know that you are just as worthy and valued in this world as everyone else, even when it feels like you aren't.
You have to step out of self-judgement and look at yourself with unconditional love, just as you do when you look at everybody else…
You have to love yourself as much and as hard as you love everybody else.

[cont...]

As the wave of unworthiness begins to recede with the tide, I gather myself, find hope once again.
Cling to it with all that I am, using it as my determination to get things right with myself and with others.
Wanting that hope to become my reality, our reality; wanting to be stronger than ever before for you and for me.

CONSISTENTLY INCONSISTENT

Depression and anxiety setting in,
body feels numb, torn again.
Why is reality so brilliantly sickening?
Wish I could go back to the very beginning.

Exhausted, I lie here waking,
my mind is anyone's for the taking,
this confusion is so mystifying.
Which direction am I going?

Why is the speed never slowing?
It all feels wrong, like I'm falling.
Surely this isn't real; am I stuck in a dream?
Settle down; calm the savage scream.

Consistently inconsistent;
I can't see the truth in your lies.
Staggered movement;
can't see through these blackened eyes.

WORTHLESS

For my worth is not mine; it is carried in the careless hands of others.

Taken for granted, bent in ways it shouldn't be in order to become self-fulfilling for them, not me.

Accused of having an agenda when looking out for others, helping others, loving others… Like I want or need or expect something in return when nothing could be further from the truth.

For I love you and want you to love yourself too; believe in yourself, stick up for yourself, stand up for your hopes and dreams…

Knowing I will be right there by your side… if you want me. And if you don't, I'll still be right there by your side… My soul, my spirit, my heart cheering you on.

I am not here for me; I am here for you. It is your happiness, your hopes, your dreams that mean everything to me, make me happy, drive me. But if you think I have an agenda in that, then there is only one way that I can show you I don't, prove to you that I don't.

And so I am working towards that... Towards showing you, showing my kids, that I am not worthless... That I think of you all the time and want to help you all achieve your hopes and dreams...

As I wait for a few final things to be sorted, fall into place, I work on removing myself, erasing myself, from people's lives... From Twitter, Instagram, Facebook. People who took me for granted and take me for granted and don't even remember me; don't remember my name. People who don't care about me, whether I succeed or fail. People who come to me with a sense of entitlement they have no right to carry and then judge me for not having that.

It's time for me to be less and less and less... It's time for me to erase myself from history, what hasn't already been erased by others, that is... Whatever is left will be gone so I am untraceable, so I cannot be found. Ever.

[cont...]

One final update will be made before I disappear to ensure those people in this world I cherish the most have a claim to everything I own; that they are looked after in my absence. That they are looked after until we meet again in the clouds.

Because while I am not worthy here... While everything I write or produce or share or say is never seen or heard, always ignored by those whose opinions matter the most, one day I will be seen, be heard.

While I am perceived to have a self-centred agenda... It is simply not the case, so it is time for me to step up and show everyone once and for all that I only want what's best for them, no matter what it costs me.

And so that is what I'll do... For it is at least a legacy to those who matter to me. And one less thing for them to worry about.

REALITY IS SHIFTING

Caustic agenda,
decadent days.
Fear within me
grows with pain.

Lasting affects
of what I've become.
Can you hear the screaming?
Do you feel numb?

Who am I, where am I,
what am I doing?
Somebody tell me,
help me keep going.

Reality is shifting,
understanding is hard to grasp.

ANXIETY PANDEMIC

My heart beats 80 times a minute,
and I wonder what that means
in this strange new world…

How 80 people's lives
have just changed forever.

How 80 families will
never be the same again.

Anxiety rises…

My heart beats 100 times a minute.
The news has begun; again.
The same pandemic, only the numbers are higher.

100 people sick,
now it's in 100 suburbs.

100 countries lose control
in 100 days since it started.

Anxiety rises…

My heart beats 120 times a minute.
My temperature rises, I choke up,
wondering how long before it catches someone I know.

I sit, short of breath, wondering if it's got me!
How did I get it, who did I give it to?

But I know it can't be
when no one's left the house in three months.

But still…

Anxiety doesn't fall…

WHITE WASH

When we left, the sky growled at the wind as it howled back
before the clouds turned into a waterfall,
filling my backpack as it drowned me.
The journey now controlled by the current falling from the sky.
Pushing me forwards towards the distant mouth of the vast ocean…
Eventually…

Out of control, I pass port, pass trees, pass houses, pass in and out…
Walking on water, no path in sight,
it's like the Suez Canal with no boat, the Dead Sea come to life!
All I know is that I have no idea where I am,
where I am going, how long it will take to get there
on this stream to nowhere.

The 'we' we once were when we left now 'I',
left scattered from the party I once travelled in.
The valley now a raging river between two mountains,
scenic walls that refuse to release the white wash.
Me, the buoy left bobbing up and down, down and up,
gasping, clinging onto what I can, yet slipping away.

Now home is gone,

        it just floated past;

                the TV antenna

                        it's satirical mast.

BANG!
BANG!
B
A
N
G
!

Your mouth fires invisible bullets no one sees,

your hollow point words penetrating

my mind,

my heart,

my soul.

UNWORTHY

More vulnerable, more exposed than I have ever been in my life; so much given, so much taken.

Crushed, my heart is like a doormat; dirty and trampled.

Destroyed, my soul is like the surrounding dirt, haphazardly scattered from pillar to post.

Drowning myself in gin, in wine, in pain.

Hoping, waiting for the onslaught to stop; the relentless blows that leave my eyes swollen and my face raw as I'm curled up on the floor, rocking back and forth, screaming in silence as my mind and thoughts destroy me.

Angry at my life and all I have lost.

Angry, always, at myself, blaming myself for the decisions others have made for me; always sorry, forgiving them but never myself.

For I am not worthy of care or compassion from me or anyone else.

I am not worthy of forgiveness. I am only worthy of blame.

For if I give all of myself, my heart, mind and soul, and it's never enough yet always too much, that's no one's fault but mine.

In the numbness, in the heartache, in the pain, I hate myself. In these moments, I realise how unworthy I am of anyone's time or care, unworthy of even the fastest fleeting thought.

So why should anyone care about me if I don't care about myself?

Why should someone care about my life when I'm numb and roaming, lost in the enormity of the universe, alone?

For it is anyone else who's more worthy and important than I.

Everyone else who's so much more deserving of their hopes and dreams.

And I will do all I can to help them achieve their hopes and dreams, no matter what it takes from me.

CHAOS

I thought that I could talk to you about what afflicts me.
But it's clear I was wrong, guess you've got your own needs.

This night is blacker than black to me, so dark that I can't see.
                Wish this would go away, that I could be set free.

Where is everything I once believed in?
Is it inside me, hiding, seething?

            Breathless, I seek clean air, but keep drowning in dirt.
            How much longer will this go on; the torment, the hurt?

This chaos is so haunting,

                              this life, so very daunting.

I thought I could trust you,

                              but instead, I disgust you.

MEMORY

I am nothing more than a memory you sometimes think about.
A person who's passed through your life
left heart broken, soul destroyed.

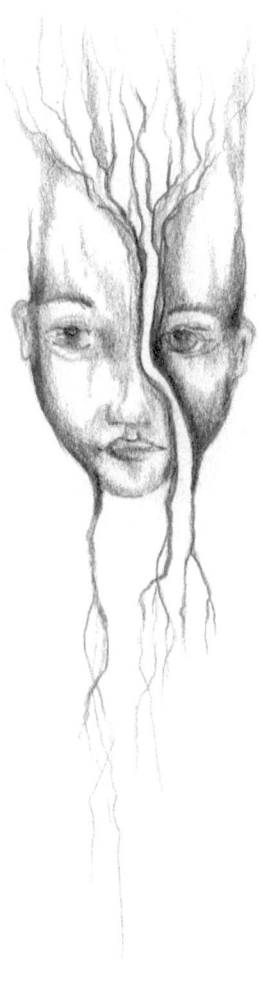

PUSH ON

When you send something that's never answered,
when you say something that falls on deaf ears,
when it feels like it's the end when it's just started,
do you push on or hide in fear?

When being yourself is misunderstood,
but a short time ago, it was seen as good.
When adapting to all of life's circumstance
leaves you gobsmacked, wanting, in a trance.

When reality hits like a brick wall to your face.
Replaying your life back in your head, your mind's displaced.
When you've seemingly become a burden that no one wants to bear,
curled up in a ball screaming, scratching, ripping out your hair.

When your heart's been ripped from your chest and served on a plate,
you try so hard to make it right, you hope it's not too late.
When it all comes crashing down, and you don't know what to do,
your mind is racing, never stopping, full of demons that feed on you.

How do you push on?

To what do you hold strong?

SORRY

I'm sorry.

    I'm sorry I'm not enough.

        I'm sorry I was never enough.

            Know that in my insignificance,

                you are so much more than enough

                    and I love and appreciate you for all that you are.

                I want you to know and never forget that.

                You, your beautiful heart and mind and soul,

            deserve so much more than my unworthiness,

        so much more than me,

      for I am clearly incongruous.

    I am sorry for trying.

I am sorry.

VISIBLY INVISIBLE

I cannot function, cannot fight,
but I can sure screw things up alright.

I cannot move, cannot breathe,
but I can hurt those I love most, aggrieve.

The shame for those who know me is no mystery,
as they begin to erase me from their history.

Special moments captured in time are deleted,
leaving my sense of worth and value depleted.

Broken and deflated, my shell pushes on,
left emotionless, empty, lost, gone.

Left fighting so hard for everybody else,
but no one fights for me, not even myself.

Visibly invisible, as it seems I've always been,
this hopelessness overwhelming, fearing sleep and dreams.

IN THE END

I hear your screams of pain,
can you hear them? They're not contained.
Quietly getting louder, seeking shelter,
as the tears stream down your face again.

Floating, falling, slipping through the cracks,
gone on too long, come to far, there's no turning back.
What has become of us, are we stuck in a dream?
Everywhere, always, nothing is as it seems.

Loving you more than you'll ever know,
even if sometimes it doesn't show.
But you can see I don't pretend,
you know it's worth it in the end.

We're stronger than we'll ever know,
that's the thing with us; strength doesn't show.
It's not like we're proud, more like we're hollow,
strong on the outside; inside no one cares to know.

...Or do they?

HEAL TO HEAR

I look into your eyes, but I can't stare too long.
It's like staring at an eclipse when the moon shadows the sun.
You are the brightest star that I've ever seen.
But invisible to you am I, as the trauma smashes me.
It stole all of my passion, all of my light,
left me in the darkness with no option but to fight
alone as I need to, to show that I am strong,
that I can heal through this, although the road is long.
See, it wasn't intentional, it's that I couldn't hear.
Trauma left me reeling, clinging, driven by my fear…
But you can't hear when you're living in fear…
Fear of losing everything that's important to you,
of perpetuating a reality that breaks you…
Until it's no longer fear…
And reality completely shatters you…
Then you realise…
That hurting people hurt people, hurting people hurt people, hurting people hurt people,
and I don't want to hurt you ever…

As I'm on my path to strength, I heed all I have learned, all that's been asked of me.
I step back to give space, I silence up.
Left beaten, battered, bloodied, betrayed, I'm still here with trust, patience, hope and love, and I will rise.
Cos hurting people hurt people, hurting people hurt people,
and I refuse to do that…

So I'll build myself back up brick by brick, by brick by brick, by brick by brick, by brick,
until I'm so grounded I am unshakeable, unmoveable, steadfast, strong once again…
Cos hurting people hurt people…
But I? I will no longer hurt…
I will heal, unwavering in my strength.
I will rise, stronger than ever…
No longer invisible, I too will now shine bright!

2 - SOUL HEAL

*"I am stuck in a perpetual cycle of
fight or flight...
Or at least everyone else flies while I
stay and fight; for them and for me."*

GHOSTS

When you paint people with the same brush

as those who hurt you in your past

instead of hearing, listening,

believing in who they truly are,

all you do is break your future.

All you do is resurrect ghosts.

BURDEN

Unworthy and useless to all I know, a burden in their eyes;
someone who's there if needed, but otherwise a waste of time.
Invisible, unheard, and silenced by those surrounding me,
seeing my importance, value, as nothing, totally empty.

"You give too much, you talk too much, you try too hard,"
                                                    they say.
But they only tell me that when they want me to go away.
Turning the burden into my own, a weight I carry every day;
never discussed or spoken, ashamed, I keep it hidden away.

But it's time to release it, set it free; it's time to rise above
all that these feelings do to me, to others that I love.
It's time to step back, learn and heal, let it go and grow,
then reconcile, repair, rebuild for those I love and know.

PTSD AND MDD

Two simple acronyms, yet to say the journey is hard is an understatement.

I have been working harder than anyone could ever know or see.

I have been clinging to my passions in music and poetry and growing those, building community, reading, writing, performing and reaching the eyes and ears of so many who have valued and appreciated my work, my support, or both.

My journey has been hard.

My journey has been lonely.

My journey has been judged by everyone.

There is not one person in my life who caught me, held me, saw me, heard me, believed in me...

Except for ME...

And now others are beginning to see, to hear, to understand that what happened to me wasn't my fault; that horrible things happen, and sometimes we are powerless to do anything about it.

That our response to our own trauma is unique, and just because one person reacts one way to a traumatic event doesn't mean that everyone reacts that same way. And just because we ourselves reacted a particular way to traumatic events in our own past doesn't mean we'll be triggered the same way again. We are all unique, and so are our stories and our reactions to those.

I have come to understand my own journey. I have come to see that it is unique to me. I have come to find peace in the way that I tried so hard to work through my trauma, my triggers, despite the judgement of literally everyone who I thought saw me, heard me, had my back.

Because the reality is that no one did...

I have come to accept the blame those who refused to see me, to hear me, decided to cast on me. That is their truth, not mine.

I have come to accept that people I believed in decided I wasn't worth the fight, turned their back on me when I was trying so hard not to drown, decided to blame me for what happened, what I was going through, how I was accused, judged and never seen or heard in that, as I tried to survive.

See, that's the thing about trauma and the relentless depression that comes with it...

It comes in waves, and no two people experience it in the same way.

No two people react to it in the same way.

And therein lies the hurt, the pain, the misunderstanding, the isolation, the loneliness...

Therein lies the unravelling...

And unravel I did... Fall apart I did... Hurt myself I did... Go through a dark night of the soul I did; in a way that I cannot describe with words. I did not think I would make it out alive. Especially when no one seemed to care either way.

[cont...]

But do you know what?

I made it; I came out the other side stronger, with more love for myself and for others. With more compassion, empathy and understanding than ever, even when those closest to me cast me aside.

Because they are worth more than the ignorance and indifference they showed me. And I finally know that I am worth more than that too.

I have worked hard, oh SO hard, on understanding, on learning, on healing, on growing. And I have finally seen that pay off...

A few months ago, I was attending an open mic. It was a great night, and I performed and was proud of how I did, especially as I hadn't had the time I had hoped to prepare. So it went well, and I congratulated all the poets who performed on a great show and left. A normal night... Until I fell asleep on the train...

And I don't sleep... But I had been especially exhausted lately, and this night, I was wiped on so many levels.

When I woke, I was past my station, and my backpack had been stolen.

My immediate reaction was to go to a bad place... A dark place... A triggered place... To relive the mugging and all it entailed, all that broke, all that destroyed.

But do you know what? While I went to that place straight up, I managed to pull myself back... I managed to sit in the moment and find a way to rationally disconnect myself from the old traumas that had been triggered. Because while it had some similarities, it was also vastly different.

And I am SO proud of the way I handled that.

It showed me that I can, will and do stand in my power, my strength, my self-belief, my worth.

It has shown me that despite the judgement of others, the empty promises of others, the blame and betrayal of others, that I am strong in their weakness, I am worthy despite their judgement, their silence, I am understood, even when others don't understand, I respect others, even when they don't respect me. Because when I needed people I trusted more than ever, I was accused, ignored, abandoned, misunderstood. And in that, I tried to understand and honour all I was asked and all I promised. I have done that and will continue to do that in actions, in words, in silence, as I have promised. Because I refuse to stand still as I heal and grow.

If you have someone in your life who is going through trauma, please take the time to really listen, really understand them and what they are going through, how they are dealing with it. It is an impossibly hard journey made harder by ignorance, indifference, judgement and silence.

[cont...]

Do not make assumptions; see them, listen to them, hear them.

Dealing with trauma and depression is debilitating enough without dealing with ignorance and judgement in silence too.

Be there for them.

Stand by them.

Believe in them.

STONE

I will cast away these stones that weigh me down, weigh us down.
We will no longer sink; we will release these stones, and we will rise.
    We...
        Will...
            Rise!!!

Higher than the highest highs we could ever imagine, fathom. Stronger than we were before, with more clarity and determination,
    compassion,
        understanding,
            respect.

The stones that have been cast away have no place here.
They have no right to pull me down, pull us down, burden us.
And I promise you they never ever will again.

For the stones of defeat will sink to the depths as we rise to the highest heights!

CIRCLING - A DAY IN THE LIFE...

I lay motionless.
Another sleepless night spent staring at the ceiling,
my blank canvas on which the thoughts in my head play out before my eyes.

I breathe deeply.
The acrid air stings my throat, burns my lungs,
reminding me that this is not a dream; that this is oh so very real.

I rise slowly.
Escaping the warm cocoon that has protected me, held me tight,
through the long cold night I thought was never going to end.

I prepare myself.
Thinking of the things I need to do, need to achieve,
adjusting my focus, finding the urge to go on, to be useful to someone, to anyone.

I look up.
Overhead, the clouds hide the sun, shadowing me in darkness, right at the time I need its warmth, its light, more than I ever have before.

I move forward.
Aspiring to be the best me I can be, finding others,
and in doing so, finding myself, listening, helping, seeking to
be better.

I look back.
Reflecting on all that I am and all I hope to be; my truth.
For I'm not just here for me, I'm here for you too, no matter
how much it sometimes hurts.

I start again.
This vicious circle…

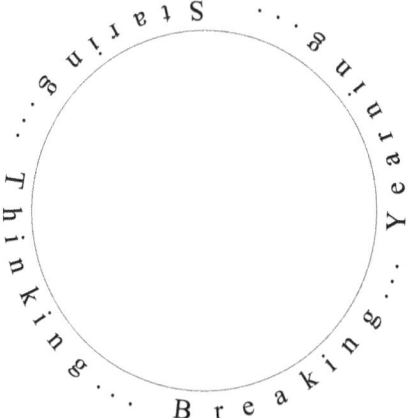

NOT ALONE

I walk to my car,
unlock the door, start the engine.
The headlights magically ignite, shining a light on my loneliness, my darkness.
A song begins playing on the radio. I recognise the voice, the song…
I have heard it before, but never like this…
The lyrics flood me with feelings and emotions of missing people I love,
yet who no longer care if I am here or not.
Places that matter to me, that are important to me,
yet places where I no longer seem to fit.
The powerful lyrics make me ponder who really cares, make me wonder when will I find where I fit in?
Overwhelming feelings triggered while sitting in a car at night listening to music…

Strange, isn't it?
Cos they nailed it!
How do they know these feelings of loneliness?
So intense, so overwhelming, so destructive.
How do they know the sense of loss?
Of someone who means so much, who you've been there for,
yet who turns their back on you in your time of need.
Someone who you would fight for, die for,
whose side you are on forevermore, no matter what.
Someone who no longer hears you or sees you,
yet you still hear them, see them, fight for them.

Strange, isn't it?
How people can turn on you in a heartbeat.
How they can simply forget every word they said, every promise they made.
One minute they say they love you; the next they poison you with their words,
and rip your heart out like it's a weed in their garden.
And yet you continue to fight for them,
stand by their side, love them unconditionally
with no expectation of anything in return.
Because all is not as it always seems,
and even those we know best can be fighting beasts and battles they don't share.
So they turn their back cos they don't see another way.

Strange, isn't it?
How in the grief, in the loneliness,
there is hate…
Yet hate solves nothing, so you let go.
There is resentment…
Yet resentment solves nothing, so you let go.
There is loss, oh so much loss!
There is running, there is hiding.
Yet there is searching, there is love, there is hope.
When will I find where I fit in?
When, not if.

[cont...]

Strange, isn't it?
How artists like this who go through stuff,
and write stuff and share stuff the only way they know how,
connect with us at our most vulnerable,
at our most exposed,
in our most painful moments.
And yet this is the point!
A timely reminder,
that we are understood,
that we are seen, that we are heard.
That despite how we feel, we are not alone, never ever alone.

And in those moments, that is the most important thing to hear and to know.

WHEN

When you ask someone a question, but get no reply.
When you thank someone for something, but see only sky.
When you apologise for something and it falls on deaf ears.
How does it make you feel, your hopes and your fears?

What can you do to fix it, what can you say?
A friendship takes two people, it takes longer than a day.
It takes two people to want it, to need it in their life.
If only one can see it work, it only leads to strife.

My heart breaks as I watch this dissolve before my eyes.
My mind takes every ounce of energy I have to calm its lies.
Missing the past, hating the present, wondering what the future holds.
Hiding all this inside myself makes me feel so alone and cold.

Persisting despite these feelings, knowing the goal is worth the pain.
Consistent in my love, my care, despite it appearing all in vain.
Trusting in the universe, that it knows what is true, is right.
Believing that there's more here, that it's important, worth the fight.

BLEEDING HEART

Your forked lies stab me like truths, every one puncturing a little deeper.
I sit in silence as my heart bleeds out…
But that's it's job, isn't it?
What's wrong with me?
Why am I not worth defending, fighting for, understanding, when everyone else is?
Why am I worth nothing more than being turned on in my time of need?
I am stuck in a perpetual cycle of fight or flight…
Or at least everyone else flies while I stay and fight; for them and for me.
I am left mute, trusting people that betray me, but I can't even see it.
I reflect on the lies that people tell themselves to make them appear right; feel righteous.
But to blame someone else to feel better is never right.
Shutting out, shutting up and shutting down deals with nothing.
And I get it; some people just want someone else to blame so they don't have to look at themselves.
They live in their history, assuming everyone's the same as those from their past.
Blaming others instead of listening; so much that they break their future. But not everyone's the same, so never paint them that way, because that's not fair on you or them.

Because you don't know what someone you love is going through if you only assume.
If you tell them you see them, won't hurt them, but never hear them and simply walk away.
If you demand respect but never see it as something that needs to be given too.

But I will not buy in. I have too much respect for you and for me.
I have too much respect and honour to break a promise I made with you.
You are so damn close that I feel your breath, yet I can't see you, touch you.
But that doesn't change the fact I'm a brilliant rainbow,
and no one has the right to steal my colour or my light.

40

Being new is daunting, but being here a long time is just as bad.
Settling down into a rhythm, yet speechless and sad.
Not knowing people, yet knowing them, can be so hard to do.
This I never really realized, until I met you.

Sometimes life is unpredictable, good intentions can be false,
but with you and me, our hearts on our sleeve, open and honest.
Sometimes I mistake your silence for something I have done,
but then you'll ask a random question, and I know there's nothing wrong.

I am gonna miss you if you go, please tell me it isn't so.
I am gonna miss you if you go, and I know it's the end of the road.

Sometimes your sense of nervousness, it does worry me,
but in this house of rumours, your concern I clearly see.
Just so you know, I don't care what they say or they think.
That's just my cadence, friendships too real to watch sink.

I trust you more than you know, with things that burden me.
I hope you trust me with your burdens too, so I can help set you free.
Things we say go no further, and this we both know.
Opening up can be hard, but for your sanity give it a go.

Know it's not the end for us, my friend.
Time will go, and our friendship will grow.

Where to next for you? No one even knows.
I just want to see you happy, content, achieve your lifetime goals.
If that means it's your time to move on, I wish you all the best.
But selfishly I hope you stay, that this place frustrates you less.

I am gonna miss you if you go; Please tell me it isn't so.
I am gonna miss you if you go, but our friendship will still grow.

WHAT IS THIS?

What is this, don't even know.
Happening so fast, but it should be slow.
What is this? It's scaring me,
yet I must stand tall, do what's best for them and me.

When something unexpected throws you off your guard,
when something you completely missed hits you hard,
when someone tells you something you never thought you'd hear,
do you stand up tall and face it, or run away in fear?

You'll never know how much it ended up hurting me that day,
when you sat down and blamed me, then stood up and walked away.
I thought this was the start to a beautiful friendship,
but instead, it's all so broken; broken mind, broken spirit.

I am who I am because of experiences in my past.
I deal with things differently so that friends and friendships last.
That might seem selfish, but it doesn't mean I don't care.
I care too much, and sometimes that is what's not fair.

I think of you every day, just like I do my other friends,
but now things are so very different, seems it's come to an end.
I think taking all the blame would make you feel much better now,
fix things, sort this broken friendship out somehow.

What is this, don't even know.
Happening so fast, but it should be slow.
What is this? It's scaring me,
yet I must stand tall, do what's best for them and me.

GOOD BAD

My eyes have not seen rest for many days now.
Been here before and functioning as only I know how.
One foot in front of the other, keep moving forward,
no turning back, just stepping through many a closing door.

I have lost whatever control I thought I had.
It's not a good thing, but it doesn't feel that bad.

This has been a hell of a year for me and those I care for.
I just want them to be okay; I just want to make sure.
Been focussing my attention outside of me and didn't see
what was going on right before my eyes, what's happening to me.

When did I forget that I am here too?
When did I stop, to myself, being true?

How can I better balance the way that I am?
How can I be a better friend, a better man?
Be aware of others' feelings, but think of mine as well
so that we can all together power through this rough swell.

LOST AND FOUND

I was looking for a friend today,
I lost one the other day.
I don't know what happened and I don't know why,
but all I could do all day was sigh.

Meanwhile you were there, caring for me.
You wanted to make sure I was fine, I could see
that I was making it worse than it needed to be.
And then I realized you were the truest friend to me.

They say friends are there in your time of need,
help fulfil your hopes, help fulfil your dreams,
but that's never really been something I've seen before,
until the day I walked through this new door.

You will never know how much it means to me,
our catch ups, conversations, coffee and tea.
I hope that I do return the favour to you,
cos friendships work both ways, I know that's true.

I was looking for a friend today,
and you were right there in my face.
It's the littlest things that you do,
that make me feel special, better for knowing you.

PUBLIC SILENCE

I sit on the bus; the single chair cos no one is there.

Away from other passengers, I have clean air to breathe,

a 1.5 meter invisible cube for my anxieties to relax in.

Silence   fills   the   space   between   stops.

Not a normal silence; an awkward one.

One where there should be much noise;

passengers talking, traffic all around.

But there are few passengers, little traffic.

And in these crazy times,

that's the way I like it.

WHERE DID YOU GO?

Where did the true you go to
when the drugs took a hold on you?
Where is the friend I used to know?
Why was it your time to go?

We used to be close a long time ago,
but now you are someone I don't even know.
What started you down the path you chose?
Where are you now, nobody knows?

The things you say, are they false or true?
Is it the drugs talking, or is it you?
Some of the crazy stuff you write is scaring me.
For our own good, it's best I set you free.

It hurts so much to see you like this.
I tried to help, could see something amiss,
but you pushed me away in your drunken haze,
said you'd never bother me again for the rest of our days.

If only you loved yourself as much as you loved me.
None of this would have happened, you could be free
to live your life, to be happy and content,
but cos of choices made that's not the way things went.

Why did you make the decision to end it all
and not to clean up your habit or give someone a call?
I blame myself; I wonder what I should have done,
but it was your life, your choices that left everyone with none.

So I'll focus on the positive memories of you.
It's all I can do to get me through.
For what it's worth, I'm sorry that you felt you had to go,
but that's what you wanted; God rest your soul.

SILENT SCREAMS

I know that it was hard, what you were going through.
An impossible decision, the one you chose to do.
Depression and anxiety stole everything from you,
but with your lad-ish attitude, no one even had a clue.

I wish there was something I could have done
to change your mind so you could meet your daughter and her mum.
Those you have left behind, each living their own hell.
And every single day, they want to wish you well.

What were you thinking?
Why didn't you share your pain?
Bottled up, you kept on drinking.
Your silent screams were all in vain.

I wonder every day what you are thinking now,
sitting up in heaven, tenderly looking down.
If you had your time again, would you still choose to do the same,
knowing the legacy you left behind when someone hears your name?

We try to focus on the good times, and yet we still feel sad.
Your determination to see everything through, whether it was good or bad.
We know you're there even when we don't know what to do.
Every time the 'Family' catch up, we all know that you're there too.

MISSING

Good times, bad times, we had them all.
Then suddenly, without a sound, things just stalled.
Was it your fault or was it mine?
Or was it the hand of things divine?

Things happen for a purpose, that is what life is,
nothing's changed, still the same, like we never split.
Why did it work out this way? I don't know.
Guess we've each been drifting in a boat we couldn't row.

> Missing me missing you.
> Missing you missing me.

Look where we ended up, we each have our own lives,
other significant others, offspring that bring us joy,
but we still have each other to care and help along,
making sure we remain friends, keep on going strong.

INNOCENCE SCORNED

Innocence scorned like a thorn in my side.

Nowhere to run, nowhere to go, nowhere to hide.

Situations are wasting me away.

How I wish for a new day.

Searching through the cracks appearing in my life.

Seeking an alternate route to keep me out of strife.

FEARLESS

I gave my everything to them all
even when I had nothing left to give.
But all they did was shrug, gave my emptiness
a name, and told everyone but me,
then they turned their back and ran away,
their silent dust clouds, haunting me 24/7,
as I saw no-one but dusty ghosts wherever I turned.

But I am done being a martyr, a scapegoat.
I'm done explaining myself to those with
no eyes to see, no ears to hear.
Those who justify treating people like
they are buried under the ground
they walk on so they can walk all over them;
so they feel better, validated in their own ignorance.

Those whose mouths fire words at everyone's ears,
filling them with targeted lies in an attempt
to murder my truth, desecrate my soul.
Yet when it comes to me, all they do with their gun is silence it;
blame it for having a trigger they knew they shouldn't pull,
but they pulled it anyway.
And it makes me think…

Just because you show love, doesn't mean you'll be loved.
Just because you give compassion, doesn't mean you'll receive it in return.
Just because you choose to listen, understand, respect doesn't mean others will.
Just because your strength is softness, doesn't mean you are strengthless.
Just because you have fear, doesn't mean fear has to have you.
For there is courage in fearlessness, power in softness and strength,
and I will stand firm, no longer hiding from their loaded guns.

Because just like their actions, they are full of blanks!

WAKE UP

Wake up, wake up, wake up, this is not a drill.
This is not another one of your cheap thrills.
Beaten down by those who are always at your door.
Stuck in a place between hell and the floor.

You feel like you have been used for so long.
You know in your head that that's so wrong,
but you can't seem to change; help is who you are,
even if those closest seem to go too far.

Staring in from a distance, you see the light.
Reminds you, guides you, inspires you to fight,
for what you believe in, for what is true,
even if it means they still hurt you.

QUARTER TURN

One day, life will all make sense,
but right now, in its present tense,
I am lifeless and roaming, lost and alone,
holding onto a hope that I must atone.

Every day leaves me in suspense,
one day, life will all make sense.
Until then, I'll keep searching low and high,
turning my eyes upward towards the sky.

Seeking to be the best me I can be,
living, learning, growing, healing for me.
One day, life will all make sense,
until then, I'll chill out, be less intense.

Approach all things with an open mind,
searching, learning, seeing what I find,
relax, stay calm, let down my defence.
One day, life will all make sense.

STRONG

The worst part about being strong is that no one asks if you are okay…
They turn to you, lean on you, depend on you, rely on you.
But when you need the same, they turn their back and walk away.
Use you, turn against you, reject you as a waste of space, too much yet never enough.
Which makes me think…
If someone is okay with losing you, going back on every word said, on every moment shared,
did they ever really care for you anyway?
If someone asks something of you and you listen, honour that, only to be ignored, blamed, ghosted,
did they ever mean a promise they made, a word they said?
Were they ever there for you? Or were they only there for themselves,
taking all they needed and wanted at their timing, their choosing. Then throwing your generosity, your belief in them, your unconditional love for them, back in your face when they were done.
Blaming you for everything that has ever gone wrong.

EVER.

See, I might look strong…
But behind the smile is sadness…

A thousand thoughts spinning in my head until I collapse in a heap from the dizziness that remains when they turned their back and walked away.

One day, someday, I hope someone will ask me how I am.
Truly ask because they want to genuinely know.
Not out of politeness.
Not because they feel obliged.
Not because they think it's expected of them or assumed.
But because they genuinely care, want to know, just as I do when I ask someone the very same.

And when that day comes, I hope and pray they listen to the answer with love,
        with care,
                with kindness,
                      with compassion.
With the intent of standing by me, holding me, just as I hold them, even when they leave.

But until that day, I will continue to try and be at my strongest when I'm feeling at my weakest.
Because strength doesn't come from what can be done; it comes from overcoming the things you thought you couldn't.
So I will push myself to be the strongest version of me I can be, cos no one else is going to do it for me.

ADAPT

I get told that I fit in, yet it does not feel so.
The confusion I feel is breath-taking, but humility is low.
Sometimes things are not as they seem to be; that's problematic for me.
Do I trust too easily in what they say, only to be betrayed?

Am I too self-critical to what's really going on?
Am I too weak-minded to be any kind of strong?
Is the world I'm immersed in swallowing me up alive?
Can't stop giving up fighting with what's going on in my mind.

I can taste the fear in my sweat. Should I run, or should I stay?
I have to stick around, but I don't have to play
the stupid game that's going on, despite the fact I haven't been here long.
Emancipate myself from this reality. Like nothing's changed, continue along.

Need to cut through the muck and see what reality exists.
I must relax a little, so I can feel the bliss
of being part of something vital, bigger than myself.
Instead of wallowing, know people do care; it's better for my health.

Adapt to the things surrounding me,
adjust my views, focus on what I see.
Follow the tides of life, so I can protect myself.
Don't fall for lies sitting on another's dark shelf.

Adapt, don't change.

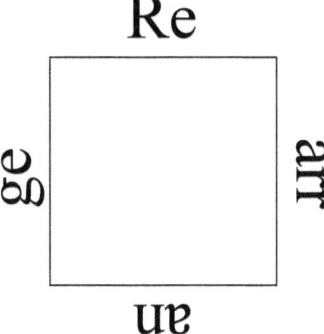

FALL AWAY

My heart is bleeding out
as forked lies stab it over and over
with the truths they led me to believe;
the truth that they would always be there,
that I could call on them in my time of need,
that I am family, and they would stay…
My heart is bleeding out;
but that's its job, isn't it?

Its echo reverberates in my head.
Thump… Thump… Thump…
The same sound the slamming door made
when they turned their back and left
right when I needed them the most;
Someone… Anyone… "Thump…" Nothing…
Its echo reverberates in my head;
silence, loneliness, the sound of my new normal.

I miss them more than they could ever know.
But love does not die easily, and mine is unconditional.
And yet that is so very misunderstood by others
who can only love with conditions, with control.
Yet even in the missing, in the loneliness,
in the pain and breaking of my bleeding heart,
I miss them more than they could ever know.
And I remain loyal should they ever need me.

There is strength in softness, softness in strength.
And despite everything, I am strong.
I needed to lose everything to realise
that I am everything I need and more.
That unconditional love just is, without
expectations, conditions, reciprocation.
There is strength in softness, softness in strength.
Anger and revenge always fall away to unconditional love.

CAUGHT BY A DREAM

Falling...

But from what?

Air rushing through my hair as I plummet,
the skin of my face tingles, the speed at which I fall pulls it tight.

The ground gets closer and closer.
There is nothing I can do.

I hold out my arms as I descend fast,
trying to glide, to slow down, yet accepting that I can't.

Not far now... The surface of the sea is close.
Need to break the surface right; I hope that the water's deep.

3, 2, 1 ... GASP! ... I sit straight up, panting for air;
hot and sweaty from the recurring dream that has me falling.

Caught by it once again.

Saved from the impact.

IGNITION POTENTIAL

Your actions show you think my worth
is no bigger than a box of matches.

But you have no control over
the potential of my fire inside.

I AM ART

I am a speck in the universe.
My voice loud as I scream my heart out to the moon and the stars,
the only things that ever hear me in my darkness, yet they show me the way, always stay.
Each experience flashing before my eyes, as I clutch at the good, process the bad,
lament in all things loved and lost, missing moments and people as I heal, regrow.
Knowing nothing happens by chance, each experience important and divine in timing,
just as the stars in the sky were scattered, yet precisely placed in their prominent position
on the canvas of the galaxy.

I am fire and ice.
Silence broken with the crack of a flint as the lighter fires.
Staring at the flame, my eyes frozen in focus, melt as the tears stream down my face in my own silent vigil to my pain, a self-sacrifice as
the flame licks my skin before the smiley of self-harm burns into my arm.
Each scar unique, like a snowflake, capturing the pain that fades into my skin
as time melts it away. Yet like a dot-to-dot, I can connect them all,
painting a picture of all that broke me; that made me.

See, I am a person.
I am more than the sum of the things that hurt me, that broke me.
Regretting nothing, respecting everything, holding space for everyone,
because I am worth it, and so are they. Sharing the good and the bad,
the inside and the out, using every ounce of strength to hold myself up on the wall for everyone to see. Sharing all I've learned, how I've healed in the hope that it helps someone,
saves someone, gives someone a new perspective. Far from a perfect picture,
I'm torn apart by wounds and bruises, held together by scars and stitches.

But despite everything.

I am uniquely me.

And I am art.

3 - SOUL GROW

*"I am lost in the silence between
ticks of the clock.
Only when the tick is heard,
am I jolted back to life."*

MIND vs HEART

An open letter from my mind to my heart...

1. When someone says they are there for you, put your wall up higher than ever.
    Tell your brain to ask them what it is that they want from you before you share
    any piece of your depleted love, because when that piece gets thrown back at you,
    and it will, it will be unrecognisable, bent out of shape, no longer fit.
    ... That's why it's called heartbreak...
2. When someone says they appreciate you, set the timer and start counting down
    the days until they don't. Because you have heard this all before.
    They don't appreciate you; they appreciate what you do, what they get,
    how they feel... Until they don't anymore... Until it's no longer enough.
    ... That's when they walk away...
3. When someone says they love you, ask them why and write down all the reasons.
    That way, when they suddenly turn on you, when they suddenly no longer love you,
    when that love turns violent and vicious and hurtful, you can look at the list
    and see that every single reason they loved you is now why they hate you.
    ... That's the moment your self-worth shatters...

4. When someone you love abandons you, do not chase them. That will only hurt them
and you. Leave them be and let them work through whatever it is that they
need to, cos chances are it has nothing to do with you anyway. Respect them.
Respect you. Give them time. Give them space. Hold space for them with patience and love.
… And work hard on yourself too, cos you need to…

An open letter from my heart to my mind…
1. Treat those you love with patience, empathy, honour and respect. And yourself too. Always.
2. Be patient, compassionate and kind to yourself and everyone else. Be patient and hold space for those you love. Never give up on them.
3. We are all fighting beasts and battles unseen. In everything you do, love yourself, love everyone else, even if it hurts. Your love can save a life.
4. Love yourself as much and as hard as you love everybody else.

PICK ME UP

There's no fooling me now, I've seen it all before,
1000 crazed thoughts beating down my door.
Past, present, future; can't stop the screams,
ever searching, hunting for exactly what life means.

This is the place where I hang my face,
and gently scream for you to pick me up again.

What am I turning into, why is it so?
Feel like I'm on fire, from head to toe.
Distressed and beaten, by what's attacking me,
need to turn this all around, be set free.

Stop trying to predict what is going on,
focus on getting there, reaching my goal.
Even if it hurts, makes me feel numb,
reinvent what I will become.

This is the place where I hang my face,
and gently scream for you to pick me up again.

CLOCK

Tick... Tock...
Tick... Tock...
Tick... Tock...
Tick... Tock...

In awe of time within this clock.
Sometimes fast, sometimes slow,
sometimes when I hold my breath,
it stops completely.

Yet each second, minute, hour,
contained within its consistent face
is exactly the same length of time
as the last second, minute, hour.

And I wonder...

When time stands still,
what is really stopping?

JOLT

Time slows, fractured between
what has been and what is to come.
A momentary pause, a stillness,
a forced sense of false tranquillity.
I am lost in the silence between ticks of the clock.
Only when the tick is heard, am I jolted back to life.

STORM

I hang my head and brace for the impact of
a thoughtless barrage of angry words
swirling in my mind like a tornado;
these relentless lies landing like truths.

The fury of these words like the raindrops
in a raging storm; big, loud, persistent.
Weighing heavy on my heart, my soul,
echoing over and over, resonating in my mind.

I pause, looking in the mirror, revealing tears.
I am shocked back into peace, my eyes like the
eye of the storm. I am, in this moment, safe; seen.
As the fury dissipates, I am reminded that

even in the storm there is magic...

The eye of the storm,

the consistent calm.

Be the magical calm.

LOOKING FORWARD BACK

I realize looking back at my time, that I have not always been fine.
Been close to the brink, close to the edge, but held it together, jumped back off the ledge.
Now it's time to set things straight so I can be confident, content, a better mate.
Sometimes it takes a little nudge, a fresh perspective from someone you trust.
Someone who knows you, expects better from you, who wants you to yourself be true.
Who sees potential, who knows you'll hear what they have to say, knowing there's no fear.

I'm a spot on this earth, a breath of air, a speck of dust in the universe out there.
What control do I possibly have in something far greater than my made up plans?
What's the point of dwelling on what's not real, when it has a negative impact on the way I feel?
When it has the potential to destroy relationships with those who matter most to me, with kindred spirits.
There has to be so much more to life than this, a higher level of presence to achieve a sense of bliss.

I'm trying so hard to make a change, to adjust the way of thinking I've had for all my age.
I want to be the best I can ever be, for my friends, for my family, but most of all for me.
It's time to stand up to the voices I hear; it's time to ignore them, treat them like they aren't there.
It's time to stop writing, turn over this page, start writing again about my new age.

It's not going to be easy, that much I know. But it has to happen now if I want to grow.
Come down from the clouds, ground myself in the present. Grasp reality firmly, love it like it's heaven sent.
No matter what is happening or what I'm going through. Take the good with the bad, learn from it, move on too.

Looking back over things has been a lesson,
listening to others' views has been kind of a confession.
Looking forward now, I have some idea,
of what I need to do, where to go to from here.

>Live in the present,
>learn from the past.
>Trust in something bigger,
>move on from problems fast.

NOOSE

As I stand here with a noose around my neck, I reflect…
Reflect on those that have come and gone, reflect on the memories of better times.
Reflect on the uselessness I feel within myself, reflect on the impact it has on my health.
Reflect on the hurt caused to others unintentionally, reflect on the pain that's left in me.
Reflect on all I have been asked by those I know and love, reflect on my thoughts.

It's time to take off the noose, rise up…
Rise up above the unworthiness that holds me back, leaves an emptiness inside.
Rise up to meet the challenge to show I am more; I am important in people's lives.
Rise up to understand, to learn, to grow, to show I am respectful; someone people want to know.
Rise up and reconcile, move forward, grow; be the best that I can be for everyone I know.

Including myself.

WANT

I want to make everything right again,
I want to show you that now, today.
I want to show you I'm growing, healing,
I want to show you we're going to be okay.

        That faith in me is not misguided,
        I'm someone you can believe in, always.
        I hope you want to know that, see that,
        feel that, until the end of our days.

So I listen, understand and respect
you and all that you ask of me.
Knowing this is how I show you,
that I want you in my life with me.

        But this is not just my own choice,
        I know you need to want it too.
        I hope with all my heart you do,
        that in my life there'll always be you.

WALK THE TALK

Depression, anxiety, stress…
Depression, anxiety, stress…
Depression, anxiety, stress…
Depression, anxiety, stress…

Mental healthcare in this country?
Let's be honest; it's a mess!
Doc, I know I am here for the DAS test,
but your black-and-white carelessness,
your sugar-coated ignorance,
do you really think that's best?

Why is the gatekeeper responsible for my mental health hurting it so much?
What right do they have to stand between me and my psych?
How is it right that the person who doesn't understand
stands between me and the person who might?
How can they hold my life in their hands
and stop me from saving mine?

It doesn't matter what the trigger,
the problem's only getting bigger,
so they look at the stats with rigor,
generic stats, breed solutions that make us sicker,
and I think…

Your assigned risk factors are by the book,
but no two peoples' experiences are the same if you look.
See there's no index for mental health.
Just a list of terms, a glossary,
gloss over me and make one stick!
Then push me out the door, still sick.

See, I'm an eight percenter…
One of the people with a mental health condition
with two or more disorders;
PTSD, MDD, Social Anxiety.
The glossary terms they stick to me,
now part of me.

Yet leaving me walking around armed.
My triggers like those of a loaded gun,
when pulled, create an inner silent explosion.
The result? A rush of blood to my wounded mind
as my soul splits open and my emotions shatter.

But I confront my demons head on.
Because I have to.
Because I have no choice.
Because even those who understand
don't understand
don't stand by me, or even near me.
Just look the other way, walk away
and all I can do is say…

[cont...]

Don't abandon those you love in their time of need.
Don't leave them in silence.
For silence screams contempt,
contempt breeds complacence,
complacence creates indifference,
and the one's you love?
They're just left silently screaming, broken and alone.

So find your empathy and compassion.
Even when they can't care, don't care,
care for them with all that you are.
Don't show them the door; show them that you're more.
Stand behind the talk you talk and do not walk!

HANDS DOWN

Hands down, that was the best day I can remember…

As time would have it, it had to end.

Now I am lost, sad, lonely;

down,

so

down.

Only the memories linger

when I hear the song play loud, but

never am I taken back to the best day I can remember.

FAVOURITE SONG

As I walk through the grocery store, I'm oblivious to all but the shelves, my trolley, my shopping list; each aisle a groove on the record of my shopping track.

…And then. It. Happens…

The music transcends from the speaker above me, loud like it was never there, yet it always was. A melodic background until familiarity nests in my ears.

See, this time, it's different.

This time it's my favourite song.

Which is to say, when my favourite song plays, I feel nothing.

I mean, it's just a song, right?

Its subliminal rhythm, melody and lyrics cause me to reflect…

I stop, transfixed to the spot; suddenly oblivious to everything but the rhythm and melody;

the words whispering in my ears like those from a snuggling lover.

As I stand in the grocery store, I hold my breath, feel my heart race!

Yet the rest of me is still, paused as the shoppers move around me like I'm not even there;

like a needle stuck in the groove while the track continues.

Which is to say, when my favourite song plays, I feel lonely.

Missing the moments, the people, the point in time it became my favourite song.

My eyes begin to fill with tears as I am flooded with everything, yet nothing all at once.

What's happened? What's wrong with me? Why do I feel like this? It's my favourite song!

Snapped out of my trance by the polite "excuse me" of a layman who can't hear or understand the importance of the moment I'm held captive in, who sees me as nothing more than an obstacle in aisle seven.

Mind stuck in the past and the present, my body fixed, yet liquid, as I realise I'm now swaying to the song's ebb and flow.

Which is to say, when my favourite song plays, I feel seen, safe, understood, even when no one's there.

Protected in that space, that moment in time…

I wipe the tears from my eyes, begin to move once again, understanding myself better, immersed in the conclusion of both the song and of my feelings.

Which is to say, when my favourite song plays, I am the rhythm, I am the melody, I am the lyrics, and the intense emotions leave me stuck on repeat...

[cont...]

Repeat...

Repeat...

BEACHED

As my world is rocked,
I retreat to the safety of the sea.

The sand, the salt, the water,
blasts my skin as the storm approaches,
much like the careless words
and actions of those I trust;
piercing my heart,
breaking my soul.

Yet, in this moment, I am grounded.
The threat of storm damage not enough
to break my strength, my resilience.

That in the midst of both internal and external chaos,
the beach is the place where I feel safe.

CLEANSE

Words...

Words mean so much,
or nothing at all.

Words can cleanse or condemn.

Words can comfort, care and nurture,
or they can cut deep like a beast in a frenzy.

Words can bring immense happiness,
or they can cause sleepless nights.

Words can paint a picture so beautiful,
or a scene of total devastation.

Words hold so much power.

Use them positively.
Use them wisely.

Always...

CHANGE

Change is not always welcome, it is not always nice,
but it is always happening, that is a fact of life.

There is no point in running away from it scared,
that won't stop change, or keep the current sacred.

Change is an opportunity to heal, to grow, embrace it.
To do anything else is to misunderstand, misplace it.

But always remember change affects others too,
so show them compassion, just as you show to you.

REFLECTION

Looking back over my time on this place we call Earth,
every single day I've walked it, searching for why I'm here.
I ponder, what do I regret, where have I seen my worth,
what have I learnt, what are my strengths, what is it that I fear?

When I think about all these things, I'm filled with many moods.
What does it mean, is that success or failure of my time?
Happiness, sadness, calmness, anger, satisfaction too.
Always pushing myself to be better, to be sublime.

Sure I've failed; I've tripped up as everybody does.
I'm not perfect and nor are you, that's what helps us learn.
Many successes under my belt, and some failures too,
listen to my heart, my guide, for what is right, discern.

So I push on to be my best for all those whom I love,
seeking to be a better person, each new day rise above.

FUTURE

The door swings shut, traps me in this empty room

of desolation, desperation, hopelessness.

I consider all which is behind me, all I've overcome,

as the triggers that left me beaten, broken, empty,

come knocking once again...

But this trauma, this depression, has no right to hold me hostage.

No matter how hard it bangs at the door, I will not let it

come inside. I will not let it gain control of my future.

Escaping through the window, I claim my space

before it even knows it has lost its grip.

4 - SOUL SOAR

"If you could read my soul, you would discover a universe of love that you have never experienced."

IN THE ROOM WHERE I BELONG

In the room where I belong, I am safe.
Safe from myself;
from the relentless thoughts of unworthiness that grip my throat so tight.
From the sleepless nights spent woken with darkened thoughts.

In the room where I belong, I am seen;
seen by those closest to me,
with love, kindness, understanding, compassion and care,
not with the hurt or judgement seemingly always found there.

In the room where I belong, I am heard;
my voice is strong, unwavering;
always clear, not misunderstood, or twisted, nor silenced.
Never misinterpreted, taken away, ignored.

In the room where I belong, I am me,
and even at my weakest, I am strong!

NEW BEGINNINGS

After all that has happened, all that has passed,
the road that has been travelled,
deserves a new start.

A brand-new beginning, a chance to make things right,
to grasp what has been learnt, to grow,
to stand up, to fight.

For what we believe in, for what we know is true,
to make it as it needs to be,
for me and for you.

All things happen for a reason, beginning through to end.
As we look inside, reflect and heal,
trust in the process.

Start over.

Begin again.

SPECK

In the universe,

I am but a speck of dust

Staring at the stars.

RE-CREATE

When you sit and you wonder, when you try and then you cry,
when you're cut deep and it hurts you, do you run or stand on by?
When you don't know what to say or what to do,
I'll sit with you in silence, just be there for you.

Where do you go to, where do you run,
when the hole in your chest reveals a blood-red sun?
I'll be there to listen when you are screaming out,
I'll be there to carry your weight of endless doubt.

Create beauty from madness,
create healing from pain,
create happiness in sadness,
create sanity from the insane.

WHY WORDS?

Why is it words that I choose to share on a page or on a stage?

I write to help others, never to hinder.

I write to heal others, never to hurt.

From my deepest, darkest places, I write so that others can see light;

feel seen, heard, understood.

But…

Be careful with words, for they can cut like a knife or save a life.

Be wise with words, for what is helpful to some can be a weapon to others.

Be clear with words, for sometimes they need a little more explanation.

Always choose your words wisely,

and deliver them with love and care.

JOURNEY

Some are long, some are short,
everyone's journey is different,
even if they are on the same path.

The feelings, the experiences,
all unique to the individual,
interpreted by them alone.

But sometimes it helps to share,
to talk, to discuss them with another,
who is on a similar journey.

To understand, to learn, to respect,
the perspective of a-trusted-nother.
To heal, to mend, to grow.

To appreciate a similar journey,
from a new perspective,
point of view.

SOULED

Hello. Who are you?
When did we meet? Why are you here?
Where did you find me? What were you looking for?
How did you hide your fear?

I am so thankful you came along, my friend; I hope you feel the same.
For me, you arrived just in time; my mind needed a reframe,
a reminder of who I am, my deepest darkest me.
And here you are to show me, to set me free.

When you dwell out on the fringe, it's hard to see the light.
It's a constant uphill battle, alone you seem to fight.
So I'm glad our paths have crossed, my friend, our souls have finally met.
Side-by-side for life's long journey, to that there is no threat.

To have met someone like-minded is so positively surreal.
Who sees the unseen in me, things which subconsciously reveal
through cracks that may appear, through a subtle change in words.
To have someone who can see that is to finally be heard.

Now we turn to each other to face our lives each and every day,
knowing we're always there for each other, we're who and what we say.
We walk through life now hand-in-hand, through both daylight and night's cold,
knowing you are here and I am here, forevermore, together souled.

PROMISE

A promise kept, a promise broken.

A promise hidden, a promise spoken.

A promise, a moment frozen in time.

A promise, a hope, a vision, a sign.

JOURNEY OF THE SOULED

Our beautiful journey is not over; this I know with all my heart and soul. It's too important to us both to get this right, too important to let go.
Please know I have only ever seen you, heard you, loved you as best I can. But I have fallen short, I'm not perfect, I'm a broken man.
Just know that I am always here to catch you if you fall; to be a shoulder to cry on, to be your rock, your wall.
Not in co-dependence, not an escape, but with tender love and care; knowing I will listen, I am safe, always there.

I know what I need to do to step up and protect all we are, and I promise to always do that, no matter what, where, near or far.
Depth over distance, souled to the end! So much more than just words, I'm your very best friend.
Someone who is here through the good times and the bad, even in the silence, even when you're sad.
I am here if you want me to listen, to help you and us to heal. Just know you aren't alone, even in the silence, our vibe I feel.

The roots of our souled friendship are deep and strong and true, even when the storm breaks the branches of our tree.
But the storm will calm, as they always do. The broken branches will grow back unbreakable, stronger than before.
So I hope we can restore faith and trust in each other and ourselves; bring our amazing friendship back to good health.
Loving, caring, understanding, healing and nurturing all we are.
Best Friends, always and forever souled, the core of what we are.

Please never forget how talented and important you are, that your heart and mind and soul will take you so very far.
Please never forget who I am, all we have gone through, the memories that remain; constantly growing on this journey together, learning, never in vain.

I need my souled best friend to know how much I love them.
I need my souled best friend to know how much I care.
I need my souled best friend to know I'm thinking of them.
I need my souled best friend to know I am always there.

TWIN FLAME

As we emancipate our minds to this beautiful mess,
we stumble together, overwhelmed, confused.
An intensity, both profound and heartfelt,
our unique and energetic connection rare.

A deep unexplainable bond formed in an instant
through vibes unseen, thoughts not shared, yet
known and understood, feelings sensed in moments
where words are not enough to express reality.

This continued to grow when we met face-to-face.
Our first hug, a homecoming, felt totally right.
Through shared interests, values and beliefs,
our unique creativity sparked together as one.

No matter how near or distant our embodiment,
we see the light and dark others overlook,
perceive each other's state of mind, emotional aura,
work together to resolve the unresolved, to heal.

As crazy as it began, it continues each day.
We share thoughts, feelings others avoid
with understanding, compassion, care, respect,
defying logic, we let go, allow this to be what it is.

Relaxed in the process, our true friendship thrives
as we make sense of how integral it is to us.
A safe, reliable space, we accept, forgive and trust.
We, twin flame, no matter how far apart, will burn forevermore.

BREATHE YOU IN

I want to breathe you in.

You, the enlightened spirit to my empty soul.
You, the life-giving blood to my heavy heart.
You, the tranquil water to my vast ocean.
You, the bright shining stars to my dark night sky.

I want to breathe you in…

                              And never breathe again.

YOU. BEAUTIFUL YOU

You. Beautiful you.
You fill me up with your love til I float like a dove with the sun high above and the sea far below. No... I'll never forget, walk away, let you go.

You. Beautiful you.
You bring so much light to my life, and I bring that to you, all I am, all my worth, I offer to you, so you know I am true, I am real, I'm a person with whom you're souled, a place that you know you are always safe.

You. Beautiful you.
I love your mind, love your soul, love your heart; I'll fill the hole that's been left there by those before who came knocking at your door with their selfish hands, selfish thoughts, selfish actions that left you hurt...
Who tried to take so much of you, steal your heart, steal your soul, steal your love, steal your worth, left you scarred, left you crying in the pain that was all that remained when they walked away.

But you. Beautiful you.
You are so much more than any of that.
You are so much more than all of that.
You are strong, you are courage, you are real, you are raw, you are YOU!
You are filled with a drive, a determination to strive beyond all that's been cast in your way on your path.

You are more than their actions, than their hurtful words, than their attempts to break you through their actions, their words. You are more than the ghosts of your past that don't last; that you want to forget, but your mind won't let you...
Beautiful you...

So what do you do?

You. Beautiful you.
You take all your pain, sit in it and drain on the page with a pen like a gun in your hand. Take them down one by one, push the clouds, pull the sun. Brighten your life and help others hiding under their covers of hopelessness, shame, help them push it away, know that they're not alone, so they feel better and glow. Every person that reads you, that sees you, that knows you, makes the world brighter as they feel validated, feel lighter.

And I...
I will love you on your bright days, your shadow days, your nonchalant days. I will love you in silence, in distance, in written words, face-to-face, soul-to-soul.

I will always love you unconditionally. I will always be here for you, ready to be by your side, to catch you if you fall, pick you up, dust you off, hold your hand, heal your wounds.
To remind you just how beautiful and important you are; to me, to so many, to the world, to the stars.

[cont...]

You...
Beautiful you...
Lovely you...
Precious you...
You are the brightest star that shines from afar, bringing light to the night in the darkness, where we fight the thoughts and feelings inside, bringing clarity and clearness to the pain within us. Your beautiful heart and mind and soul helping those who hurt to feel whole, to feel strong once again.

You. Beautiful You.
You are the brightest star.
Never ever stop shining.

PRECIOUS PIECES

"I'm sorry for everything that has ever hurt you," I cry out.

The pain you feel, I feel, bleeding from the same wounds that afflict you.

"Know I am deeply sorry, but know I am patient and strong."

Believing in something far greater than me, I press on with courage.

To fight for you, for me, for what is right, for what we believe in.

I gently clean your open wounds, bandage them so no scars remain.

I help you back to your feet, steady you as you stand, walk again.

But something is still not right.

My head hangs in shame.

Then I see it, your broken heart shattered before me on the floor.

The pieces stain my fingers as I pick them up.

You look at me, wonder why I'm here.

The tears stream down my face as I put each precious piece back into place.

"I am here to mend your perfect heart with my imperfect hands."

HIDDEN

We all have hidden stories no one cares to know or understand.

So to find someone who

    sees them,

        hears them,

            listens to them,

                holds your hand,

            laughs with you,

        cries with you,

    understands,

is the most amazing honour a person can ever receive.

Cusp

Reflecting on the past,
while looking to the future;
I'm on the cusp,
of failure or greatness.

Holding on tight,
while letting go;
I'm on the cusp,
of failure or greatness.

I'm on the cusp,
of failure or greatness.

But only time will tell which cusp is my destiny.

HOME

Home is not four walls and a roof,
doors, windows, carpet and tiles.
That is a house, not a home,
the difference is enormous.

For home is where the heart is,
home is the other half of your soul.
Home is respect, understanding, love,
sights, sounds, scents, a long hug.

Home's standing strong through easy and hard,
good and bad, and everything in between.
The hot and cold, the light and dark,
together growing and learning.

Home is a person, your tribe.

Not a building.

COURAGE

I look up at the moon,
wonder if you see it too;
looking at me, looking at you.

Lost in time, staring at
a clock that's blinking 8s,
I haven't slept in so long.
My sleepless nights are
now my bitter oblivion.

I'm fine, just tired,
and hiding from things I can't
contain or explain.

But I am trying.

Harder than anyone sees,
harder than anyone knows,
to stay encouraged.

To stand in courage.

RISE

As I stare into the mirror, your hands reach for me,
casting my hair aside so you can hold my face close,
look into my eyes, stare into my soul.

I have been lost, alone for months now, oblivious to time,
as I float to the distant shore of healing, strings of trauma
trying to pull me back as I fight.

While the waves have been tidal, sinking me at times,
I now float in the calm, the shoreline in sight,
pausing in my thoughts as the current pushes me forward.

The strings cutting, stretching, breaking,
as the winds of change pick up,
I am no longer a puppet to the trauma that broke me.

No longer floating, drifting, being pulled by strings up and down,
left and right. Now knowing my soul is held as I'm mirrored
back to myself, grown, flying higher, as I rise.

SONGTENSITY

No matter where I am
when those special songs play,
they take me back to a moment,
a time,
a person,
a place.

Consumed by the music, the lyrics,
I travel to those moments in my life;
the people I cherish most.
Some are here,
some are there,
some are not.

In that moment,
I feel the intensity of the memory created
when each song was added to the playlist of my life.

FROM DAD, WITH LOVE

Words cannot describe how proud I am
to have you two sons, my amazing little men!

It's not always easy; life never is,
but our little wolf pack's always strong,
always partners in humour, prank and fun.

You are both always there when no one else is,
loving me the only way you know how;
unconditionally and with all your heart and soul,
and the tightest hugs going around.

You see more than others give you credit for,
you feel more than others see and do.
They all treat you both like little children,
but with knowledge and insight, a maturity beyond
your years, there's so much more to both of you.

Through the way you see the world, the way you embrace it,
your poems, anecdotes, insights, your words and statements.
The music that never ceases to be sung from both your mouths.
The passion you hold, your belief to overcome self-doubts.
Your empathy, compassion in everything you do,
the way you share that with others to empower them too.

I know I am not always perfect in everything I say and do.
I can't always protect you from everything that breaks through,
that worries, that bullies, that angers, that eats away at you.
But I promise to love you, teach you, guide you, always be there
for you every day, no matter what. To show you, support you,
love you as much as you show, support, love me, and more.
I love you every day in more ways than I can say with words.

Just know I don't ever take this privilege for granted.

And each and every day, I am reminded

it is an honour to be your dad.

GROUNDING

The wind told me to listen carefully to its ebb and flow,
to stand tall and lean into it, knowing I am held,
to be still, feel its push, let it guide me to my higher self,
that I am not alone; never ever alone.

The waves brought me a message. They said
the moon and wind make them what they are;
it's what makes them beautiful, powerful,
in both the calm and the storm.

I spoke to the sand, my eyes stinging as the tears streamed down my face.
I asked, why is everything so chaotic when all I crave is calm?
It replied that the universe will give you what you need
right when you need it, that it is divine in timing.
That our choice is to listen, to learn, to grow
just as the trees do towards the light.

If you could read my skin, you would see
every beating, every battering, every scar,
every burn I have endured; by my own hands
or by the careless hands of others.

If you could read my palms, you would see
every weighted callous, every scratch, every wound that has tried
to destroy me; that's made me!
You would see every path travelled, every dead end,
every decision that led me to a closing… an opening.

If you could read my heart, you'd find peace in its pieces,
each one full of so much love, so much care,
so much truth and authenticity;
all of it bleeding out through everything I say and do.

If you could read my soul, you would discover
a universe of love that you have never experienced.
And while, at times, this has been judged by those
who don't understand as self-fulfilling,
it is everything but that. It's real and raw,
without expectation. It is me.

The sunlight said, although like you, I am sometimes
hidden behind heavy clouds, I am always here
to warm you when you're cold,
to guide you when you're lost in the darkness,
to bring you home to yourself.

And I replied…

I was lost and wandering,
But I am listening and following.
I am grateful for everything,
and I am ready to go home.

YOU ARE SEEN

Hey... You...
There in the back, standing in the shadows,
hanging your head in shame cos all you feel is blame;
I see you.

Hey... You...
Smiling, laughing, happy in the middle of the crowd,
yet totally numb when there's no one around,
lying in fright from your demons in the middle of the night;
I see you.

Hey... You...
Opening your chest and baring every wound
with an open mind and heart and soul
wanting nothing more than to help those
who need it the most;
I see you.

Hey... You...
Lying in the street in little more than the skin you were born in.
Drugged, beaten, robbed, through no fault of your hand.
Suffering more than anyone could ever understand.
The mugging, the cry for help, the resulting self-harm,
they blame you for it all, but I know it's not your fault;
I see you.

Hey... You...
Carrying the weight of everything yet feeling shame.
Relentless voices won't stop; they always victim blame!
Wanting everything to end, yet holding on tight
despite living in the darkness while always seeking light.
Overwhelmed with it all, yet completely alone,
wanting nothing more than to feel
the warm embrace of home;
I see you.

Hey... You....
You behind the microphone,
front and centre on the stage.
It took so many years to find you,
a beating that left you with nothing but PTSD, anxiety.
Being shrunk, abandoned by those that matter
when you needed them the most.
Left misunderstood, invisible, unheard, unseen
through manipulation and narcissism of those you believed in.
Breaking their view to find power, worthiness, self-love in you;
I finally see you too!

SURVIVAL

Life is a journey…

A trajectory of

ups and downs,

lefts and rights,

light and dark.

A soul refraction...

MAY YOUR FUTURE

May your future shine like the sun, giving warmth and light,
may your dreams motivate you to fight for what's right.
May your current state be full of strength and might,
as you travel on your journey, fight your good fight.

May the way you have shattered be turned into good,
may it help to guide others as you heal, burn deadwood.
Learning self-worth, self-love, reclaiming livelihood.
Sharing with others so they know that they too, could.

May your heart have the peace that its pieces desire,
resonate bright, a leading light full of heart-warming fire,
a hate-free zone full of love that no other soul can mire,
impacting humanity positively, always seeking to inspire.

No matter how far you go, may your heart find a home,
may your tribe hold your hand, may they never let go,
believing in you always, no matter how far you roam,
as you share courage and love with others, together or alone.

May your legacy leave the planet a lasting impression,
when the time comes to walk the stairway to heaven.
May your words still ring true and help long after you're gone,
when it's all said and done, may your history live long.

But until then…

May your future shine like the sun, giving warmth and light,
may your dreams motivate you to fight for what's right.
May your current state be full of strength and might,
as you travel on your journey, fight your good fight.

NOTES

Precious Pieces first published in *Anti-Heroin Chic*, February 2020.

Ghost first published in *Poetry 365*, July 2020 Ed.

Heal to Hear (excerpt) first published in *Poetry 365*, July 2020 Ed.

Lungs first published in *Poetry 365*, July 2020 Ed.

In the Room Where I Belong first published in *Anti-Heroin Chic*, August 2020.

Beached first published in *Take Heart* (PatP), 2021 Anthology.

From Dad, With Love first published in *Take Heart* (PatP), 2021 Anthology.

Rise first published in *Take Heart* (PatP), 2021 Anthology.

Fall Away first published in *Joined Up Writing - Three Fall*, 2022.

Silent Screams first published in *Calling Up the Day* (PatP), 2022 Anthology.

White Wash first published in *Calling Up the Day* (PatP), 2022 Anthology.

Thank you to those who have also shared my spoken word and page poems in the past including: Black Bough, ByMePoetryAus, UntwineMe Australia, Cooee Poetry and World of Poetry.

ACKNOWLEDGEMENTS

Thank you to everyone who has allowed me to share my words behind a microphone, be that online or on stage.

Thank you to those who have backed me, my words, and given me the privilege of featuring both on the stage and on the page. It is an honour that I am forever grateful for and never take for granted.

Thank you, Lisa and Dragonfly Publishing, for seeing me, hearing me, giving me the opportunity to get my spoken words onto the page for everyone to read.

Thank you, Neshka, for your amazing art and interpretation of both the title and structure of this book and the poems inside. You captured it all perfectly, and I am so grateful and honoured to have your art grace the cover and pages of this book.

Thank you to Natalie, Elijah and Jadon for being my constant. I would not be here without you. Thanks for standing by me, for listening. For all you endured when I was in my darkest days, I am sorry. And I am forever grateful to you and love you all. Thank you for believing in me, in the power of music and words, and for backing me and joining me on this journey.

Elijah and Jadon, please know how proud I am of you and how honoured I am to be your dad every single day. Thank you for being my biggest fans and inspiring me to never give up on the power of my words. Thank you for showing me this every day through the power of the words you write and share.

Thank you to my friends and family for being there, for holding me up when I could do nothing but fall.

Finally, thank you to you, the reader. Know that you matter and know that I hope my words help you find a new perspective, that they help you and your soul to heal, to grow, to soar.

ABOUT THE AUTHOR

Paul R Kohn is a writer of poetry and short stories, performer of spoken word, and creator of music and lyrics.

Residing in South Australia, he has featured at The Festival of Now, Mixed Bag Poetry, Spoke N Slurred and The Good Word in Adelaide, West Side Slam in NSW, Perth Poetry Club in WA, Alternator Poetry in the Gold Coast, and performs regularly at open mics live in Adelaide and online, both nationally and internationally.

Most recently placing third at the 2021 Spoken Word SA Winter Slam, he placed first at the April 2021 West Side Slam online in Sydney and first in the July 2020 Ruckus Monthly Online Video Slam in Brisbane.

His work has been published in *Calling Up the Day* (PatP Anthology, 2022), *Joined Up Writing – Three Fall*, *Take Heart* (PatP Anthology, 2021), *RDW World*, *Anti Heroin Chic* and *Black Bough Poetry*, and his work has been shared by ByMePoetryAus, UntwineMe Australia and Cooee Poetry, to name a few. His written words also won him first place in World of Poetry's 1K Instagram competition in Dec 2021.

Paul writes as a way of processing, understanding, healing and growing, and shares his written and spoken word poetry all over Australia and the world in the hope that it helps others too.

You can find Paul R Kohn on Facebook, Instagram, Twitter, Tumblr, YouTube and Soundcloud.
For details, check out Paul's website at:

https://paulrkohn.wordpress.com/about/

www.ingramcontent.com/pod-product-compliance
Lightning Source LLC
Chambersburg PA
CBHW020323010526
44107CB00054B/1952